Critters of Country Critter Farm

Come along to the farm and learn from the animals!

This book is dedicated to Sweet Pea,
as she touched so many hearts.

Written by Jessie E. Strong
Illustrations by Justin D. Swindall
Edited by Emily L. Strong

Jetta lives in the big city, but she loves to come to the country to visit the Country Critter Farm.

She likes to come help Farmer Scott with all of his critters at the Country Critter Farm.

She loves to talk to the critters and they like talking to her too.

"*Good Morning, Farmer Scott! I'm here to visit the critters and help feed them.*" Jetta says. Farmer Scott then says, "*Good morning, Jetta the critters are waiting for you!*"

As Jetta walks to the barn, Sweet Pea and Jasper walk over to greet her.

"*Well Hello, Jetta,*" Sweet Pea says.

"*Jetta, we are so happy to see you!*" Jasper adds.

"*I am happy to see you both!*" She responds.

"*Did you know most people do not understand why we are smaller than a pony?*" asks Jasper.

"It is because you are very special, remember we all look different and that is OK, I love miniature horses and I love you both. I want to learn from all of the different types of critters at Country Critter Farm."

Jetta responds.

Just then, Felix the goat walks over to them.

"Jetta, there are a lot of different kinds of critters at our farm, like how Domino is quite large, while Oreo is small and fluffy. Just like your friends at school may look different, but it does not matter. We are all important, we are all special. Now, why don't we go for a walk and see all the critters here at Country Critter Farm?" Felix asks.

"*Come on, let's all go together.*" Sweet Pea shouts

back to them, as she begins towards the barn.

 Meanwhile in the barn there is lot's of voices and

shouting.

"*Hey Everyone, our friend is coming to see us!!*" All the

critters shout with joy!

Suddenly they hear, "*Oink oink,*" "*Quack quack,*"

"*Gobble gobble,*" and a big, "*Cocka-doodle do!*"

All the critters gather around Jetta.

Hershey the dog wants to join the fun too! Here she comes barking into the barn tail waggin', "*I want to learn about all of you too.*" she says.

Penelope and Petunia say, "*Oink oink, we are also different from Puddin,*" and Puddin sitting beside them says, "*Yes we are different.*" Penelope then continues to explain,

"*We are Hereford Pigs, you can tell by our color and the marks on us. Did you know we can grow up to 600* pounds? We also like to play in the mud to cool off.

But Puddin is a Razor Back Potbelly Pig."

Puddin adds, "and I am a boy and boy pigs are called

Boars. As you can see, I have tusks, but do not worry

about them... I am very friendly and I like belly rubs.

Some of my cousin's even live in people's houses."

Little Arnold wattles up to the front of the critters,

and in his tiny voice says, *"Hi there!"* As Jetta picks

him up, Arnold continues, *"Thank you for loving me,*

Jetta. I am so grateful for you, and for Farmer Scott.

Being the smallest pig I sometimes get afraid, but everyone helps me."

Rocky the rooster then lets out a loud "*Cocka-doodle-doo!*" and puts his wing around Chicken Ginger, then adds, "*I am the king of the coop, I wake everyone up when I crow. I wake up Farmer Scott*

every morning and then he comes out to say, 'Good

Morning, Critters!' and then he gives us fresh water."

Ginger adds, "*The other chickens and I lay lots of eggs*

for Farmer Scott. As you can see there are many

different sizes, shapes and colors of chickens here at

Country Critter Farm.

So the eggs we lay look very different sometimes.

Some are big, some are small, and some are white, while some are brown."

Ruby Red and Mr. Red anxiously wait to speak, they are very friendly turkeys and like to follow Farmer Scott all around the farm.

Ruby Red announces, *"I lay eggs too! My eggs are bigger and have spots on them."*

"In the Spring I like to spread my feathers and walk around to show how special I am... but really Jetta we are all special in our own way." Mr. Red explains.

Oreo and Domino hop to the front.

Oreo then says, "*I am just a small rabbit, but I'm called a Lionhead Rabbit because of my fuzzy head. Lions are fierce, so even though I am small, I am not afraid.*"

Then suddenly Domino adds, "*Hi Jetta, I know I seem big, but that's why they call me a Flemish Giant Rabbit. I can grow really big, some might even say I look like a big fluff ball.*"

"*Quack quack quack,*" says Gary the duck. "*I am so happy to be here, Farmer Scott saved me from a scary place... It was dark and cold there, I had no food or water. He gave me a safe home and I have lots of*

friends here now. Always remember Jetta, everyone should care about how they treat others and never hurt or mistreat anyone."

Jetta responds, *"Yes, Gary you are right, and I am so glad you are here now at Country Critter Farm and safe. But why do you just waddle across the yard and quack when Farmer Scott comes around?"*

Then all the animals almost at once say, *"Oh Jetta, we do not want Farmer Scott to know we talk to each other or that we can understand him, it is much more fun this way."*

"*Oh look.*" Jasper exclaims, "*Here comes Farmer Scott, and look at that big horse walking with him.*"

"*Hey everybody when she comes into the barn let's all make her feel welcome; we all know what it is like to be the new critter on the farm and to not know anyone.*"

Farmer Scott and Bubbles walk into the barn.

Farmer Scott then says, "*Hi, Everyone.*"

Farmer Scott sure does love all the critters at

Country Critter Farm and he talks to them

everyday... Little does he know all the critters know

what he is saying.

Bubbles then introduces herself, "*Hi Everyone, I know I look big to you all but don't worry, I want to be your friend.*

I would never bully anyone because that is wrong."

Then all the critters on Country Critter Farm begin

laughing and playing.

Farmer Scott looks confused.

Hershey wags her tail and just looks up at Farmer

Scott smiling. Hershey knows the critters are having

fun with him.

Jetta then cries out, "*Oh no, the wind blew the gate open! Farmer Scott, there goes Penelope and Petunia running and playing all over.*"

All the critters watch Farmer Scott chase the pigs

Penelope and Petunia all through the yard as they

run and play. Joyfully snouting, *"Oink oink oink."*

Puddin looks at Jetta and says, "*They like to enjoy life when the gate is open and go as far as they can through the paths.*" Bubbles adds, "*Jetta, run after your dreams like someone left the gate open, always*

with heart and determination. Never let a gate, a fence or anyone stop you from being happy and running after your dreams."

Jetta then says, *"Thank you all, I have learned so much from you, but I think I better go help Farmer Scott."* Jetta then walks outside, calling after Penelope and Petunia to come back into the barn. The two of them turn and see Jetta, so they walk right into the barn with her.

Farmer Scott is then wondering why he had to

run after them, but Jetta did not have to. All the

critters begin to laugh and say, *"See Jetta, we like to*

laugh and live life like someone left the gate open."

Jetta adds, *"Well that was fun."*

Just then, Rocky the rooster lets out a big "*Cocka-doodle doo*" and says, "*Jetta would you like to learn more about some of the other critters here at Country Critter Farm?*" Jetta, as excited as ever, cries out, "*Oh yes Rocky, I would, and who are we going to go and see first?*"

Rocky replies, "*How about we go and see Zoey? She is a Potbelly Pig like Puddin, but Zoey is a girl. Zoey is also our only deaf animal here at Country Critter Farm. Being deaf means she cannot hear like we can, but she knows when we are near her, even if she is not facing us, by our scent.*

She also can sense the movement of someone in her house. She also loves carrots, let's take her some."

Rocky continues to tell Jetta as they walk towards Zoey's pen, *"Just like there are some people who cannot hear, there are some animals that cannot hear, but we all need love and to be cared for."*

"*Oink oink oink,*" says Zoey, "*Hi Jetta! Thank you for coming to see me, and thank you for the carrot, I really do love carrots!*"

Just then, off in the distance everyone sees Farmer Scott walking with yet another horse. All begin wondering who she is. As Farmer Scott comes closer he begins, *"This is Patches, she is going to be a part of our family now."*

Jetta notices that Patches has a patch over her right eye and then asks, "*Why is there a patch on her eye, Farmer Scott?*"

Farmer Scott then explains, "*Well Jetta, Patches had an infection in her eye once, so the Veterinarian then had to remove it. So our friend Patches, now only has one eye. She has done very well with one eye though, and she just wants to be friends with everyone.*"

Jetta then says, "*Farmer Scott she is so pretty and such a lovely color, I sure do love to watch the horses run and see their manes blow in the wind.*"

All of a sudden, there is another "*Cocka-doodle doo,*"

but wait, that is not Rocky! Jetta then exclaims,

"*Wow, I have never seen a rooster like that! He seems*

so different and he looks like he has a poofy feathery

ball on top of his head!"

Rocky explains to Jetta and says, "*Yes Jetta, there are many kinds of roosters. You see, I am called an Olive Egger because of my colors, and over there is Peter and Polly. They cannot see above their heads because of the feathers and do not perch high like other chickens and roosters do.*" Jetta then says, "*I did not know there were so many different kinds of roosters!*

So does this mean there are all different kinds of chickens too?"

"Yes, Jetta." Rocky explains. "Here at Country Critter Farm we have all kinds, we have Olive Eggers, Polish, Bantom, Leghorns, Silkie and even Wyandotte. We are all different sizes and colors.

The chickens here are all very friendly. Snowball here is a Silkie, and Polly over there by Pete is a Polish Chicken."

"It is so much fun learning about all the critters here at Country Critter Farm, but I know that it's almost time for all of you to eat, so I am going to help Farmer Scott feed you." Jetta says.

All the critters begin to make noise as they see Farmer Scott coming with the buckets of food.

"*Jettttaaaa*" Farmer Scott calls out for her. "*Would you like to feed the chickens and the goats first?*" he asks.

"*Oh yes.*" Jetta responds with glee.

Farmer Scott and Jetta then make sure all the

animals are fed. Farmer Scott then says to Jetta,

"Thank you for your help feeding all the critters here

at Country Critter Farm."

Jetta then replies, "*Thank you, Farmer Scott for having me. I love all the critters here at Country Critter Farm!*"

She then heads back to the city and dreams about

the day that she can return to Country Critter Farm

to visit all of her animal friends again. As her animal

friends rest easy, knowing that they are all special,

safe and loved.

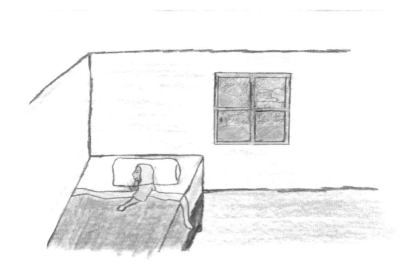

The End

Made in the USA
Monee, IL
24 December 2020